Original title:
Laughing in the Leaves

Copyright © 2025 Creative Arts Management OÜ
All rights reserved.

Author: Gabriel Kingsley
ISBN HARDBACK: 978-1-80567-316-3
ISBN PAPERBACK: 978-1-80567-615-7

The Happy Canopy Chorus

Underneath the bending trees,
Squirrels dance with such great ease.
A crow cracks jokes upon a limb,
While sunlight makes the shadows grin.

Pine needles tickle at my toes,
Each rustle brings a smile that grows.
Chipmunks giggle, chasing tails,
As breeze-born laughter lightly sails.

Whimsy Amongst the Branches

A robin sings a silly tune,
While chipmunks juggle acorns soon.
Leaves caper like a playful sprite,
Turning the day into pure delight.

Dancing shadows play tag and tease,
Nature's antics flow with ease.
Breezes whisper cheeky rhymes,
Creating joy in perfect times.

Revelry in the Underbrush

Hopping frogs play leapfrog near,
While bees buzz tales you want to hear.
The grass tickles as we run,
Giggling friends, we bask in fun.

A hidden path where secrets weave,
Where laughter bubbles, none can grieve.
Wildflowers join in on the glee,
A vibrant scene, as bright can be.

Mirthful Murmurs

In the thicket, breezes jest,
Leaves ripple like they know best.
A fox with flair prances about,
While laughter dances all throughout.

Tiny bugs with tiny pranks,
Chase each other in leafy ranks.
And when the sun begins to fade,
The forest chuckles, unafraid.

Bright Moments in the Woods

Squirrels dance in bright attire,
Chasing tails like tiny fire.
Twisting, turning, all around,
Nature's giggles, joy unbound.

A rustling brush, a cheeky tease,
A bird drops seeds like autumn leaves.
Laughter slips through branches tight,
Echoing in the soft daylight.

Happy Unfoldings

Butterflies flutter, colors flash,
Bouncing blooms, they dash and clash.
Jokes unfold among the ferns,
Whispers tickle as the breeze churns.

A frog leaps high, a silly sight,
Splashing water with pure delight.
Mushrooms giggle in the sun,
Nature's comedy has just begun.

Vernal Verses of Glee

New buds open with a cheer,
The sun awakes, the sky is clear.
In every nook, a grin can hide,
Joyful sprouts in a vibrant tide.

Puppy paws in puddles splash,
Chasing shadows with every dash.
Laughter trills through rustling leaves,
As nature's jester gently weaves.

Silly Shadows

Tall trees bend with playful bends,
Mimicking the way life wends.
Shadows stretch and wiggle wide,
Joining in the fun outside.

A playful breeze whispers a pun,
As crickets play the evening's fun.
Laughter drifts, the stars align,
The woods are joyful, pure, divine.

Tickling Treetops

Whispers dance on breezy wings,
Swaying branches make us sing.
A tickle here, a giggle there,
Nature's humor fills the air.

Bouncing leaves, a playful tease,
Chasing shadows with such ease.
Round and round, the branches sway,
In this joy, we'll laugh and play.

Joyful Echoes in the Woodlands

Amidst the trees, the echoes call,
Laughter bounces, one and all.
Dancing shadows, lively scenes,
Joking whispers between the greens.

With each step, the forest plays,
A comedy in sunny rays.
Chirping birds join in the fun,
Celebrating under the sun.

The Sound of Happiness Rustling

A rustle here, a giggle there,
The sound of joy floats through the air.
Branches bend with playful grins,
Nature's jest, where laughter begins.

Swaying trunks like dancers prance,
Encouraging us all to dance.
With every breeze, a jolly cheer,
In this woodland, we hold dear.

Chortles Among the Branches

In the boughs, a chorus bright,
Chortles weave through day and night.
With every leaf that shivers light,
A comic spark, a pure delight.

Laughter trickles down like rain,
Popping jokes from every grain.
Among the branches, spirits soar,
In this forest, we want more.

Serenade of Sundrenched Shadows

In the dance of sunlit sighs,
Whispers twirl where sunlight lies.
Jolly breezes, slight and spry,
Tickle branches, oh my, oh my!

Chasing giggles through the trees,
Nature hums with joyful ease.
Swaying limbs in bright parade,
Bring forth chuckles unafraid.

Flitting shadows, gleeful play,
Swaying softly day by day.
Gifts of warmth and laughter blend,
Where tender moments never end.

Kites of Laughter Above the Scattered Tones

Oh, the frolic in the sky,
Kites that dance and twist on high.
Swinging low, then soaring free,
  Holding secrets just for me.

Each gust brings a burst of cheer,
Chasing clouds, it's crystal clear.
Colors gleam with wit and glee,
  Painting tales on canvas, see!

Rustling leaves join in the fun,
Their soft humor bright as sun.
As we roam with hearts ablaze,
  Life's a riddle, life's a maze.

Euphoria Amongst the Falling Foliage

A tickle from the autumn air,
Secrets rustle everywhere.
Golden champions glide and sway,
Joining us in this grand play.

Underneath the whispering trees,
Truths unravel with gentle breeze.
Crimson bursts, a playful sight,
Spirits soar, oh what a flight!

Each leaf drops with a giggly cheer,
Creating memories held dear.
In their dance, we find our way,
Grateful for this bright ballet.

Heartstrings Played by Nature's Hand

Underneath the sky's embrace,
Nature strikes a heartstring's grace.
Cackling currents, sweet and bold,
Unfold the joy that never grows old.

Branches sway to laughter's tune,
Beneath the bright and smiling moon.
Rustling echoes, whispers wild,
In every breeze, we're nature's child.

Tickling toes through grassy meads,
Joyful hearts find friendship's seeds.
On this quest where merriment thrives,
We dance together, joy arrives.

Jubilant Rustles of Woodland Whimsy

In the woods where shadows dance,
Squirrels chase in wild prance,
Acorns tumble, what a sound,
Joyful chatter all around.

Leaves pirouette in the breeze,
Whispers float like teasing bees,
Bouncing branches, what a sight,
Nature beams with pure delight.

Swaying to Nature's Playful Melody

Branches sway, a silly tune,
Hopping deer beneath the moon,
Bugs create a raucous band,
Life's a laugh, just as planned.

Colors flash in vibrant show,
Wind drafts tease, they come and go,
Bark bits giggle, leaves chime in,
Here's to grins that never thin.

A Tapestry of Glee Beneath the Boughs

Frolicking fawns in the sun,
Each twist and turn, a spark of fun,
Mushrooms peek with funny hats,
Swaying softly, acting as bats.

In a patch of dappled light,
Nature's joy takes airy flight,
Twirling vines with silly grace,
Bringing smiles to every face.

Giggling Amidst the Gold and Red

Crisp leaves scatter, ticklish sound,
Pigeons strut all around,
Chirps and caws weave through the air,
Nature's jesters, bold and rare.

Pumpkins grin in fields of cheer,
Harvests bring us close and near,
Beneath the trees, let laughter reign,
In every rustle, joy remains.

Ribbons of Joy Entwined in Twigs

Amidst the rustling, laughter swirls,
A dance of colors, nature twirls.
Nutty squirrels dart with glee,
As I chase them, wild and free.

Crimson whispers from above,
Tickling ears like a playful dove.
Branches bow with a jesting cheer,
In this festival of the year.

Giggling leaves in a breezy bed,
Caressing dreams that twirl in red.
Each flutter a chuckle, light and spry,
As autumn's giggles paint the sky.

Wonder blooms where shadows play,
In every twig, a joke at bay.
With nature's canvas, here we stand,
Joyful moments, oh so grand.

The Playful Palette of Autumn's Kiss

Sunlight drips from branches high,
A mischievous wink from the sky.
Golden rays catch crisp delights,
As laughter leaps on breezy flights.

Pumpkins grin with a twisted smile,
Scarecrows pose, striking with style.
Each chuckle echoes through the trees,
Nature's humor, a playful tease.

Twirling leaves in a frolicsome race,
Spinning tales with their gentle grace.
With every swirl, a giggle sounds,
As joyfulness in this beauty abounds.

Whirlwinds dance in a lively play,
Rustling secrets in a quirky way.
In this cascade of vibrant hues,
The heart finds laughter in autumn's views.

Sunshine's Warm Embrace

Beneath the sun's bright gaze,
The giggles of the day,
A dance among the branches,
Where shadows skip and play.

Squirrels race with tiny feet,
Chasing dreams of stolen seeds,
While dandelions bloom with glee,
And tickle all the weeds.

Crickets chirp their funny songs,
As butterflies join in the cheer,
Each petal whispers secrets sweet,
That only flowers hear.

With every rustle in the breeze,
A story bursts to life,
Of laughter caught in golden rays,
And joy without the strife.

Childlike Merriment in the Glade

In a realm where shadows dance,
With laughter in the air,
The trees join in a silly trance,
And giggle without care.

Marshmallow clouds drift by,
They tickle the sun's nose,
While fireflies start a winking game,
As the night sky glows.

The leaves conspire in a rustling hush,
To tell tales of the day,
Where every twist and turn, a rush,
Of whimsy on display.

Bouncing balls of childhood dreams,
Roll through the forest green,
With every tumble, every scream,
A joyful, carefree scene.

Treetop Chuckles

High above in leafy nests,
The laughter starts to rise,
Silly birds in feathered vests,
Put on a big surprise.

The branches sway in gentle arcs,
As raccoons play their game,
A leafy comedy of quirks,
Where none are quite the same.

Mice wear hats made out of moss,
And squirrels strike a pose,
With every twirl, they laugh and toss,
Their stories, all in rows.

From canopy to forest floor,
The merriment ignites,
Each chirp and chortle, what a score,
Of nature's funny sights.

Whispers of Autumn's Joy

In the crispness of the fall,
The colors paint the earth,
With every crunch and every call,
A joy that speaks of mirth.

The acorns bounce as if to chat,
In cheerful, silly tones,
While pumpkins wear their hats so flat,
Amidst their leafy thrones.

A carousel of swirling leaves,
Whirls in delightful glee,
They twist and spin like playful thieves,
And dance for all to see.

The air is filled with laughter true,
As friends gather around,
To share the tales that nature drew,
In autumn's humor found.

The Cheerful Flutter

Breezes tickle every branch,
Silly shadows do a dance.
Squirrels giggle, frolic fast,
Time seems to spin, joy unsurpassed.

Sunlight bounces, playful gleam,
Nature hums a merry theme.
Tiny critters paint the scene,
Chasing dreams where laughter's been.

A Canopy of Grins

Leaves play peek-a-boo with the sun,
Round and round, we laugh and run.
Chirps and chuckles fill the air,
Smiles abound, with joy to share.

Mirth cascades from high above,
Sprightly whispers, tales of love.
Branches sway, a jolly sight,
Laughter glows, igniting light.

Jest in the Jungle

Monkeys swing with cheeky flair,
Swinging wildly, without a care.
Lizards wink, with mischief rife,
Every corner holds a life.

Vines tangle in a playful mess,
Jokes made up, we must confess.
The jungle sings a catchy tune,
While we dance beneath the moon.

The Forest of Joyful Whispers

Whispers twirl through leafy halls,
Tiny giggles, nature calls.
Pinecones tumble, laughter flows,
Every pathway, humor shows.

The sun peeks in, a wink so sly,
Beneath the boughs, we laugh and cry.
With every step, a whimsical sound,
In this realm, joy knows no bound.

Murmurs of Mirth in the Meadow

Whispers of giggles float on the breeze,
Among the tall grasses, the spirits tease.
Squirrels in jackets run to and fro,
Chasing their shadows, putting on a show.

A butterfly winks, flits on her quest,
Tickling the daisies, they giggle, distressed.
Rabbits roll over in playful delight,
As the sun sets and the stars twinkle bright.

Echoes of Elation in the Glade

In the heart of the woods, a chuckle resounds,
As woodland critters dance 'round and around.
Leaves rustle softly, a slapping of wings,
The joy of the forest, oh, the laughter it brings!

Frogs wear small hats; they croak with great flair,
Sharing old tales while basking in air.
The brook joins in, with a bubbling trickle,
A symphony of giggles, a joyful tickle.

Tickled by the Treetops

Up high in the branches, where the whispers run,
The leaves twirl in joy, catching rays of the sun.
A woodpecker knocks out a rhythm so sweet,
While the branches shake hands and tap their own beat.

The squirrels are jesters, acrobats on high,
Leaping from limb to limb, they glide through the sky.
The sunbeams join in, a bright, warming laugh,
As shadows weave stories on the forest's path.

The Joyful Symphony of Fall

In hues of orange and gold they swirl,
Leaves tumble and giggle in a jolly whirl.
The pumpkin parade struts down the lane,
With cackles and chuckles, they're never mundane.

Crisp air carries the scent of spun dreams,
As acorns conspire with mischievous schemes.
Nature's own orchestra, a comical sound,
Where laughter and colors in harmony abound.

The Giggle of Greenery

In the forest's gentle sway,
The branches dance and play,
Each rustle sings a tune,
Underneath the silver moon.

Squirrels dart and spin,
Chasing tails, they grin,
With a pop and a puff,
Nature's laughter is enough.

The flowers sway with glee,
As buzzing bees decree,
A joyful waltz begins,
In this land where fun never thins.

Leaves tickle and tease,
Carried on the breeze,
Each giggle echoing near,
In a world that knows no fear.

Jovial Journeys through the Trees

Venturing down the trail,
With pockets full of tales,
Every step holds delight,
In the glow of morning light.

Branches stretch and yawn,
Greeting the bright dawn,
A chorus of chirps arise,
Beneath the vast blue skies.

A chipmunk takes a leap,
With antics oh so deep,
Rolling on the ground,
In silly circles found.

Paths twisted and turned,
With each corner, we learned,
To giggle with the trees,
In moments that tease.

Lighthearted Leafy Conversations

In a circle, leaves do chat,
Amidst the sounds of splat,
Whispers shared with flair,
In a dialogue so rare.

"Look at me!" a leaf shouts out,
"Twirl and spin, without a doubt!"
The laughter starts to rise,
As sunlight paints the skies.

From twig to branch, they share,
Secrets only they can bear,
The breeze carries their words,
In songs like cheerful birds.

Blowing in the playful air,
Each flutter a vibrant flare,
Nature's humor thrives and plays,
In these joyous, leafy ways.

The Whimsy of Woodland Wanderings

Strolling through the woodland thick,
Every corner hides a trick,
A pathway lined with smiles,
Where joy travels for miles.

From the underbrush, a hare,
Winks and hops without a care,
A peek and then a show,
As wildflowers begin to glow.

The trees are painted with joy,
Each branch a laughing ploy,
With creatures that caper and dive,
In this land, we come alive.

The sun drips golden cheer,
Dancing shadows draw near,
Every wander, a sweet jest,
In this forested fest.

Rhapsody of Rust and Radiance

Colors swirl in a dappled dance,
Flickering bright, they take a chance.
Whispers ride the crisp cold air,
Nature chuckles without a care.

Squirrelly antics, quick and sly,
Chasing shadows, oh my, oh my!
Giggles ripple through the park,
As leaves pirouette, a merry lark.

Footstep crunches, a hapless slip,
Sprightly winds cause a playful trip.
Giggling ghouls in a leaf-filled sea,
What a sight, come laugh with me!

Joyful echoes of rustling cheer,
A kaleidoscope of fun draws near.
Each twist and turn, a vibrant tease,
In this carnival of autumn breeze.

The Arboreal Antics of Delight

Branches sway, a playful show,
Underneath, the laughter flows.
Conspiring winds whisper a jest,
As creatures play, they are the best.

Dancing leaves, a merry crew,
Forming shapes, both old and new.
A ruffled brow, a darting glance,
Nature's jesters in a trance.

Chirps and chuckles fill the air,
Woodland friends join in the dare.
Bouncing through the golden haze,
With every twist, the folly stays.

A tumble here, a flutter there,
Joy wrapped tightly in the air.
With every fall, a smile ignites,
In this woodland realm of silly sights.

A Galley of Grins Tucked in Branches

In tangled boughs, mystery lays,
Beneath the shade, joy's little plays.
Surprises rustle, a chuckle erupts,
Nature's whimsy in joyful cups.

Tiny critters plot and scheme,
In whispered chuckles, they align a dream.
From fluttering wings to skittering feet,
Every moment, a comic treat.

A playful bounce, a leaf-sail glide,
Joyful noise we can't abide.
Around the trunks, laughter weaves,
A tapestry sewn with autumn leaves.

With a wink of sun, a dance ensues,
In playful pranks, we find our muse.
So gather 'round, let's share the cheer,
In branches high, mirth is near.

The Merriment of October's Embrace

Golden hues in a sunlit chase,
Filling hearts with a warm embrace.
Grins explode like popping corn,
In this season so richly worn.

Pumpkin patches, hilarity reigns,
With bobbing heads, joy entertains.
Children tumbling in a bright array,
Each giggle sparks the autumn's play.

In laughter's echo, spirits soar,
Through swirling vests, they'll dance and roar.
Rusty treasures strewn about,
Whisked away with a playful shout.

Mirthful nights with playful flares,
We find delight in what each shares.
In this frolic 'neath moonlit skies,
With smiles reflected in all our eyes.

Sprightly Shadows

In the park where shadows twist,
Squirrels dance without a tryst.
Leaves chuckle as they sway,
Creating joy in the day.

Friends gather, laughter shared,
With every joke, no one spared.
Even the breeze seems to tease,
Nature's fun, a gentle breeze.

Watch the clouds, they play pretend,
Bouncing high, not wanting to end.
As sunlight sprinkles with glee,
Moments of pure ecstasy.

In every corner, joy does bloom,
Even raindrops hum a tune.
Under trees where spirits run,
Every heartbeat sounds like fun.

A Symphony of Smiles

A chorus echoes through the air,
With giggles twinkling everywhere.
Birds join in with songs so bright,
Creating joy, pure delight.

The sun winks from above, you see,
Casting shadows playfully.
Children chase with laughter wide,
As butterflies take a glide.

Grass tickles toes, oh what a scene,
Nature's humor, always keen.
A dance of colors, bold and free,
Everything grins in harmony.

In the breeze, a whisper sings,
Even the flowers sprout tiny springs.
Together we share this mirthful space,
A symphony of smiles we embrace.

Giggles and Greenery

Amidst the trees, a secret game,
Where laughter echoes, never tame.
Greenery sways to a hidden beat,
Every step feels like a treat.

Bushes chatter in leafy tones,
While playful gnomes dodge sticks and stones.
Sunbeams splash like paint on skin,
All around, the joy within.

Ants march by in silly lines,
Each one carries tiny signs.
Dewdrops giggle on petals light,
Morning's cheer, so pure and bright.

Among the blooms, a prankster lies,
With a wink and mischievous eyes.
In this place where laughter grows,
The fun is found where nature flows.

The Laughter of Nature's Quilt

A patchwork forged from joy and cheer,
Whispers telling tales we hold dear.
Every flower a note in song,
Threads of laughter, all day long.

In sunlit spots, dreams take flight,
Comedic shadows dance in light.
With every breeze, a giggle sways,
In nature's quilt, we lose our ways.

Caterpillars wiggle, what a sight,
They draw the laughter, pure delight.
Crickets chirp, a playful tune,
Keeping company with the moon.

Nature weaves a fabric bright,
Woven tightly, day and night.
Amidst the trees, the joy ignites,
A laughter quilt, our spirit bites.

Whispers of Jolly Trees

In the sun-drenched glade, shadows dance,
Branches sway, giving nature a chance.
Squirrels chatter, a scampering spree,
With acorns bouncing, oh, what glee!

A chipmunk jokes, tail high in the air,
Tickling the breeze, without a care.
Leaves confide secrets, soft and light,
Nature's giggles, taking flight.

Breezes whisper, full of delight,
Wobbling branches, a comical sight.
Each rustle and chuckle, a playful tease,
Tickling the heart, putting minds at ease.

Underneath the boughs, joy's never far,
With every rustle, we laugh at the stars.
Nature's show, a vibrant spree,
In this jolly grove where we're all free!

Giggles Beneath the Canopy

The sun peeks through, a golden ray,
A chorus of giggles in bright array.
The leaves sway gently, swish and sway,
Grinning softly, they brighten the day.

A rabbit hops, with a curious glance,
Chasing shadows, in a cheerful dance.
Frogs serenade on a lazy pond,
Rippling laughter, a joyous bond.

Branches crack jokes, they creak with cheer,
While flowers chuckle, drawing near.
Butterflies flutter, a comical crew,
Dressing in colors, a jester's hue.

In this forest, where fun doesn't cease,
Laughter echoes, it's nature's peace.
Every rustle, a wink, a tease,
Together we share in these playful breezes!

Rustling Joys

In the leafy halls where shadows play,
A fox spins tales in a cheeky way.
With every step, the leaves applaud,
Echoing laughter, a nature's fraud.

The wind whispers jokes, twisting and twirls,
Tickling the tips of the dancing curls.
A gathering of whispers, secrets unbound,
Spreading smiles in the leafy surround.

Mice scurry 'round in their little quest,
Playing at hide and seek, the very best.
Every rustle a riddle, a merry song,
Echoing through the woodlands, loud and strong.

Here in the woods, joy's the decree,
With every rustle, a giggle sets free.
Let's join the frolic, relax our ploys,
For the world is alive with rustling joys!

Playful Breezes

Along the trails where the daisies wave,
A breeze blows past, it's oh so brave.
Whirling about, like a playful sprite,
Tossing the leaves, oh, what a sight!

A clumsy bear in a rush to play,
Trips on berries along the way.
With each tumble, he chuckles so sweet,
Sharing his joy in the summer heat.

Sitting 'neath branches, laughter spills,
As sunlight glints on the hidden hills.
Giggling flowers sway with the tune,
Inviting each creature, morning to noon.

In the symphony, the nature's tease,
Every leaf quivers with playful ease.
Join the occasion, feel the release,
In this realm where we savor the breeze!

The Dance of Leafy Laughter

A breeze tickles branches tall,
As leaves shake and sway, they call.
Whispers giggle in the air,
Nature's jest, a playful dare.

Round the trees, a merry frolic,
Colors spin, a dance symbolic.
In the canopy's giggly spree,
Squirrels join, full of glee.

Rustling sound, a chuckle here,
Each leaf knows no hint of fear.
Bouncing sunbeams share the fun,
A carnival where we all run.

So come and join this leafy play,
Where joy just flutters every day.
In the dance, we find our tune,
Under the watchful, giggling moon.

Nature's Heartfelt Chuckle

In the forests, a ripple of smiles,
Branches twist and jump in styles.
Roots chuckle softly, oh so wise,
Tickling toes and teasing skies.

Frogs croak jokes from the muddy bog,
While birds share laughs on every log.
A gentle rustle rides the breeze,
Every sound brings a leaf-shaped tease.

With light so bright, the shadows play,
As laughter drifts on bright display.
Giggles burst from every stem,
Nature, the comic gem of gems.

Let's waddle through this leafy glee,
In every corner, joy's decree.
Where hearts grow light and minds set free,
In the wild, we find our spree.

Sunlight's Cheerful Murmur

When sunbeams tickle leaves at dawn,
Each shimmer holds a playful yawn.
Golden sparkles, a light-hearted tease,
Nature whispers, glimmering with ease.

Breezy giggles, twirling around,
Joyful echoes beautifully sound.
Petals dance in a dazzling spin,
Where every laugh paints a cheeky grin.

Through trees enchanted, shadows prance,
Each movement, a bright, carefree chance.
Gentle sunlight's warm embrace,
Turns the forest into a laughing space.

Come join the mirth, feel that thrill,
In this realm where laughter spills.
Under each bough, let's sway and lift,
In nature's joy, we find our gift.

Glee on the Forest Floor

Beneath tall trees, a playful shout,
Tiny critters scurry about.
Mushrooms wear hats, a comical sight,
Nature's jest in the morning light.

Leaves tumble down like confetti thrown,
In the dance of winds, they've brightly grown.
Every crackle in the underbrush,
Adds to the fun, a wild rush.

Twigs break into laughter, what a sound!
In this wild realm, delight is found.
Crickets chirp a silly tune,
With shadows playing beneath the moon.

Join the revelry, leap and spin,
The forest welcomes with a cheeky grin.
In this jolly, leafy throng,
We'll sing our hearts out, all day long.

Choreography of Crinkled Colors

Whispers in the vibrant air,
As leaves twirl without a care.
They flip and flop, a silly sight,
Dancing under the golden light.

A rustle here, a flutter there,
Gentle breezes tease their flair.
Colors clash, a comic show,
In the crispness, chuckles grow.

Twirling down from branches high,
They tumble past with a giggle sigh.
Playful forms in swirling paths,
Bring forth bright and silly laughs.

Nature's stage adorned with cheer,
Each colorful step, crystal clear.
In the vale where mirth prevails,
The crinkled colors weave their tales.

Gales of Glee Among the Branches

A gust of wind, a joyful spree,
Branches dance with wild glee.
Leaves jostle like friends at play,
In this merry, breezy ballet.

Chasing shadows, ducking low,
A playful game of peek-a-boo.
They sparkle bright, a comic hue,
In the midst of all they do.

Swaying gently, side to side,
In this natural, thrilling ride.
Nature's laughter fills the air,
As giggles swirl without a care.

Encircled by the crisp, clear skies,
The branches shake and toss their prize.
With each rustle, every cheer,
Gales of joy are always near.

The Dance of Rustling Giggles

In the orchard, breezes play,
Whirling leaves in a kooky ballet.
Rustling whispers, giggling sounds,
Joy erupts from earthen grounds.

Leaves shimmy with such delight,
Tickling the ground in their flight.
Each flap creates a punchline bold,
As laughter spins in hues of gold.

Nature chuckles, shows its grace,
A comic twist in every place.
Beneath the trees, merriment grows,
While rustling giggles steal the show.

Twirls and turns in the dreamy air,
Cascading fun is everywhere.
A festival of colors bright,
Dancing leaves, a pure delight.

Harvesting Happiness Under the Canopy

Underneath the leafy roof,
A treasure of joyous, silly proof.
Each rustle brings a happy tune,
As smiles blossom 'neath the moon.

Gathering cheer from boughs above,
The air is thick with playful love.
Every leaf a little sprite,
Dancing in the soft twilight.

Rippling laughter, light as air,
Filling hearts with warmth and flair.
Joy cascades like autumn's rain,
Harvesting giggles, free from pain.

Nature's bounty, bright and clear,
Leaves are whispers, drawing near.
A canopy of cheer proclaimed,
In this space where joy is tamed.

Nature's Playful Tapestry

Winds whisper secrets to trees so tall,
Squirrels in suits dance, ready to sprawl.
Sunshine winks with a glimmering beam,
While daisies chuckle, a whimsical dream.

Butterflies tease with a flutter and flap,
Chasing each other, a jovial map.
Branches sway gently, the rhythm divine,
Nature's own jesters in bright, frolic pine.

Rivers giggle past stones with a grin,
Splashing their laughter, a joyous din.
Hopping along is a cheerful frog,
Croaking out tunes like a comical bog.

Under the arch of the playful sky,
The beasts join in, oh my, oh my!
Every leaf rustles in humorous glee,
Nature's quilt wraps us, wild and free.

Jocular Journeys

In fields of joy, the flowers converse,
Each petal a story, a comical verse.
Bees buzz with laughter, a merry brigade,
Tickling the blooms in a sweet charade.

Clouds drift around like marshmallows bright,
Daring the sun to a tickle-fight.
Grasshoppers hop with a spring in their step,
Chasing a breeze where giggles are kept.

Paths meander, with mischief aglow,
Where each twist and turn leads to friendlier foe.
Porcupines prance in their prickly attire,
Sharing a joke by the warm campfire.

Under the stars, crickets play their tune,
As fireflies flicker, a jester's monsoon.
Nature's own comedy, full of delight,
In every small corner, life's a riotous sight.

Delight of the Dappled Sun

Sun-drops giggle on a playful stream,
Where turtles caper, lost in their dream.
Jellybeans tumble from branches that sway,
As shadows and light have a jolly ballet.

Mushrooms wear hats, adorned just for cheer,
While the wise old owl chuckles, "I'm here!"
Laughter erupts as the breezes conspire,
To tickle the leaves and inspire a choir.

Ducks skip and quack in a musical row,
With each little step, their joy starts to grow.
Frolicsome rabbits in a dramatic scene,
Playing hide-and-seek, oh what a routine!

Beneath the broad branches, they all convene,
Inventing new games that are fit for a queen.
Nature's own revel, in brightness and fun,
Tapestries woven by the dappled sun.

The Joyous Nature Ballet

Petals pirouette in the gentle breeze,
While critters twirl, moving with ease.
Dancing on feathers, the birds take flight,
Critiquing the clouds in their dazzling light.

Crickets compose with a syncopated beat,
While rabbits in tails keep tapping their feet.
Each dance is a giggle, a playful parade,
As nature conducts her sweet serenade.

The trees sway along in their bucolic grace,
Matching the rhythm of this vibrant space.
As shadows come forth, they too join the array,
In the joyous embrace of the dance in the day.

Mice in the thickets plot pas de deux,
Creating a spectacle, just for the view.
In this grand performance, there's laughter galore,
Where nature's own ballet is never a bore.

The Merry Mosaic of Nature

A squirrel in a top hat skips,
Juggling acorns with nimble flips.
The daisies bow in a hasty dance,
While butterflies twirl in a summer trance.

The brook chuckles over pebbles round,
Tickling toes on the grassy mound.
A robin sports a tiny crown,
Telling jokes to the worms underground.

The clouds drift in a cottony ride,
As wind whispers secrets from every side.
Sunbeams tickle the tulips bright,
Creating giggles from morning to night.

In this playful patch, where wild things roam,
Nature's laugh fills the air like a cozy home.
Every critter plays a part in the show,
Merry moments in the sunlight's glow.

The Cheer of the Tree-Hugger

With arms wide open, I greet the bark,
Sharing secrets with a face quite stark.
Each knot and gnarled groove tells a tale,
Of whispers and giggles that never stale.

Leaves shimmy like dancers, wearing their green,
Tickling the branches, a lively scene.
A squirrel winks from a cozy nook,
In this happy haven, take a good look.

The sun peeks through in a playful jest,
As shadows stretch out to join the fest.
With laughter erupting like popcorn pops,
Nature's delight never quite stops.

So come along and join the fun,
Where trees and joy interweave as one.
With every hug and every cheer,
Creating memories we hold so dear.

Grinning Leaves

The leaves wear smiles like masks of cheer,
Rustling softly, they draw us near.
A breeze tickles the branches high,
Sending giggles across the sky.

The flowers laugh with colors bright,
Dancing playfully in morning light.
A bunny hops with a jolly bound,
Crooning softly to the earth around.

Each shadow plays a sneaky trick,
As sunlight dances, quick and slick.
Nature's jesters in every hue,
Creating humor in all they do.

In this wild and whimsical place,
Finding joy becomes a race.
With grinning leaves and hearts at play,
Laughter echoes through the day.

Euphoria Under Boughs

Beneath the boughs, we skip and spin,
With shadows dancing, let the fun begin.
A chipmunk chuckles at our delight,
As we twirl around in purest light.

The wind hums tunes of a playful breeze,
Rustling the branches like laughing trees.
Petals flutter in a merry chase,
Nature's giggles fill this space.

Each glance exchanged, a secret code,
As the meadow blooms and joy explodes.
Hopscotch with shadows, leap with glee,
In the heart of the woods, wild and free.

Laughter lingers as day fades low,
The moon joins in with its silver glow.
Euphoria wraps us, like a sweet song,
In this enchanted realm, we all belong.

The Woodland's Joyous Serenade

In the grove, the chirps collide,
Squirrels giggle, tails like pride.
A dance of shadows, flickering light,
Nature's jesters take to flight.

Breezes whistle silly tunes,
While mushrooms sport their silly prunes.
Frogs leap high with a croak or two,
As the sun shines, laughter renews.

Puppies tumble, twigs in tow,
Chasing dreams where wild things grow.
Each rustle wraps a giggling spree,
Under branches, wild and free.

With every rustling leafy peek,
Nature shares her playful cheek.
In this kingdom, joy's the key,
With every chuckle, hearts agree.

Mirth Among the Moss

Underneath the emerald green,
Mossy mats reveal the scene.
Grasshoppers hop, a sight to see,
Tickling toes, oh, how they flee!

Among the ferns, each jolly twist,
Silly whispers, nature's list.
Trees play tricks with shadows low,
While wiggly worms steal the show.

Sunbeams play a peek-a-boo,
As gnomes giggle, just a few.
Each caper brings a burst of glee,
In this mossy jubilee.

Watch the daisies burst with cheer,
As laughter echoes far and near.
In this realm, where humor sways,
Nature's joy, in wild displays.

Giddy Moments Under the Sky

Clouds tumble like playful sheep,
While dandelions sway and leap.
A parade of smiles on the ground,
Where laughter's echo can be found.

Butterflies prance in sunny light,
With wings that twinkle, oh, what a sight!
Bees buzz along with silly hums,
As the meadow skips and drums.

Tickling breezes race around,
As petals spin, they twirl and bound.
Every moment bursts with zest,
In this haven, we are blessed.

Underneath the vast expanse,
Nature invites us all to dance.
With giggles shared above the grass,
These giddy times are sure to last.

Trees That Tell Jokes

In a circle, branches sway,
Whisper secrets, come what may.
Each bark has tales of olden days,
In puns and rhymes, hidden ways.

Swaying limbs in playful jest,
Rustled laughs we love the best.
Acorns drop like funny bombs,
As woodland creatures read the psalms.

Gnarled roots with winks so sly,
My, oh my, how trees can try.
Laughter wraps around each trunk,
In leafy green, we find the funk.

As shadows play a merry chase,
Nature creates a joyful space.
With each quirk and tree-shaped grin,
A world of giggles draws us in.

Sunshine's Playful Whisper

Golden rays dance in the air,
Tickling noses, everywhere.
Silly shadows jump and play,
Chasing giggles through the day.

Frolicsome breezes swirl around,
They trip on roots just off the ground.
A chorus of chuckles fills the space,
As nature dons its funniest face.

Every whisper, a cheeky jest,
The sun's warm smile, the very best.
With every flicker, a playful tease,
A happy heart drifts on the breeze.

Through branches wild, the fun does flow,
Jokes in petals, putting on a show.
Each turn's a spark of light and cheer,
In nature's laughter, we hold dear.

The Comedic Canopy

Above our heads, the branches sway,
Comedic antics in sun's warm ray.
Branches stretch, with silly flair,
As squirrels plot their wild, wild dare.

Leaves rustle with their punny quips,
While acorns drop in comical flips.
A bird on high does a goofy dance,
In nature's stage, all take a chance.

The breeze brings jokes that float and dart,
With every rustle, a funny start.
Sunbeams shine on nature's jest,
In this canopy, we find our best.

A chuckle shared, the world seems bright,
Underneath the playful light.
In this grove of laughter loud,
We create memories, laughter proud.

Giddy Growth

Tiny sprouts with a joyous grin,
Dancing in circles, let the fun begin.
Each new leaf is a silly song,
Swaying to nature's rhythm all along.

Petals giggle in colors bright,
With every breeze, they take to flight.
Nature's jokes hide everywhere,
In every nook, laughter we share.

With a wink, a flower blooms wide,
Rolling with laughter, it takes in stride.
Grass blades sway, tickling the ground,
In this garden, joy is found.

As roots intertwine with playful glee,
A hidden world of comedy.
Giddy moments, wild and free,
In every growth, a jubilee.

Smirks in the Shade

Beneath the boughs, a secret scheme,
Where shadows play and sunlight beams.
A dappled dance of light and tone,
That tickles hearts that call it home.

Whispers float on leafy sighs,
Each rustle bears a sweet surprise.
Squirrels chuckle at their near-miss,
In this realm of joyful bliss.

The picnic spread, a feast of fun,
With fruits that giggle in the sun.
Laughter echoes, pure delight,
In this cozy, shaded light.

As day drifts on, the smiles remain,
In nature's heart, we find our gain.
A world of jest beneath the sun,
In shaded moments, we are one.

Happy Whimsy in the Wild

A squirrel danced around the tree,
With nutty jokes, so wild and free.
The breeze played tag with every branch,
While butterflies laughed in a sunlit ranch.

The birds chimed in, a silly tune,
Tickling the air like a fluffy balloon.
A bunny rolled down a grassy hill,
Chasing its tail with a giggling thrill.

The mossy rocks wore a grin so wide,
Reflecting joy from the great outside.
Nature's laughter—it rings so clear,
In the heart of the woods, all scoop and cheer.

What silly sights the day has spun,
Among the trees, life's just begun.
In happy whimsy, we all play,
In the wild's embrace, we'll laugh all day.

Serendipity among the Foliage

A jolly frog in a leafy chair,
Croaked out secrets, with none to spare.
The wind held hands with a dappled shade,
As laughter echoed in green cascades.

Colorful petals began to sway,
Whispers of joy in the light of day.
Each rustling leaf had a secret cheer,
Tickling the hearts of all who'd hear.

A curious fox with a cheeky glance,
Joined in the fun, ready to dance.
Under the boughs, spirits lifted high,
With serendipity beneath the sky.

Surprises bloom where dreams take flight,
In this joyous realm, all feels just right.
Amongst the foliage, smiles abound,
Where laughter's the treasure that can be found.

Swaying Smiles

The grass tickled toes with a joyful cheer,
As daisies giggled with spirits near.
The sunbeams waltzed in a golden glow,
Spreading warmth to the world below.

A cheeky chipmunk made faces all day,
Encouraging friends to join in the play.
With every swish of a playful leaf,
Nature spun tales of joy and relief.

Clouds formed shapes that made us grin,
Bouncing along on the gentle wind.
The chorus of nature sang sweet and light,
In this dance of smiles, everything's bright.

Bouncing along, we sway and bound,
In the joy of the moment, new friends abound.
With hearts full of glee, we celebrate,
In swaying smiles, we recreate.

Leaves of Delight

In the park, a dance of shade,
Where sunlight glimmers, a masquerade.
Laughing shadows skip on the ground,
While silly antics in circles abound.

Chirping crickets put on a show,
As children giggle and toss to and fro.
The trees leaned in, ears perked wide,
Listening closely, a joyful pride.

With every rustle, a story told,
Of jolly capers, and laughter bold.
Magic sparkled in swirls of air,
Where the leaves of delight spread joy everywhere.

We twirled through paths where the sunbeams weave,
With passed moments, oh how we believe.
In a world of laughter, we find our way,
In the leaves of delight, we forever play.

Mirth in the Meadow

Beneath the sky, a dance unfolds,
With rolling hills, where joy beholds.
The daisies giggle, the wind tells jokes,
As butterflies chuckle, among the folks.

A rabbit hops, with a comical flair,
While butterflies tease, in mid-air they dare.
The sun winks down, with a twinkling eye,
As shadows bounce, like clouds on the fly.

Children run, with glee in their stride,
Chasing each other, the laughter won't hide.
Tickled by daisies, the grass starts to sway,
In this meadow of laughter, they frolic and play.

At the close of day, as colors unfold,
The sunset's blush, a sight to behold.
The echoes of joy, resound with delight,
In the mirthful meadow, a dazzling sight.

Sprights of the Silent Woods

In the quiet boughs, whispers abound,
With giggles hidden beneath the ground.
The leaves rustle softly, a secret shared,
As tiny sprights play, unbothered, unscared.

A squirrel in disguise, wears a wily grin,
While mushrooms chuckle, as if they can spin.
The trees loom tall, with a knowing smirk,
Watching the antics, their smiles don't shirk.

In dappled light, shadows twist and twirl,
Nature's jesters, in a married swirl.
A breeze tickles branches, a cascading laugh,
As forest creatures recount every gaffe.

The moon peeks in, with a silvery gleam,
Creating a stage for a ghostly theme.
As night descends, and dreams take flight,
The sprights of the woods dance through the night.

Uproarious Hues

In a palette of shades, hilarity grows,
With reds and greens, in whimsical rows.
A yellow sun, with a cheeky wink,
Smirks at the clouds, as they start to blink.

Bluebells chatter, their petals in sway,
While orange tulips giggle, come what may.
The garden erupts, with a riotous cheer,
Each blossom a rascal, spreading good cheer.

With daisies whistling, a tune in the air,
The violets join in, with laughter to share.
As butterflies flutter, in playful pursuit,
The melay of colors becomes their cute suit.

In every hue, a laughter alive,
Nature's canvas, where silliness thrives.
The flowers unite, in this joyful spree,
A vibrant display, of sheer lunacy.

Echoes of Playfulness

Between the hills, where echoes resound,
Mirth dances lightly, spinning around.
The playful whispers, traverse the space,
As giggles bounce off, every warm face.

Children's laughter, like musical notes,
Flow with the river, in tiny boats.
Chasing the echoes, round every bend,
With every soft giggle, the fun won't end.

A flutter of wings, as birds take flight,
With chirps like jokes, they delight the night.
The breeze carries tales, of innocent fun,
Where echoes of joy, dance under the sun.

As shadows grow long, but spirits stay bright,
The joy of the world, a sparkling sight.
With laughter a thread, weaving hearts tight,
In echoes of playfulness, everything's right.

Nature's Smiling Face

A breeze tickles the trees, so sly,
Squirrels dance with a gleeful cry.
Sunbeams play hide and seek, you see,
While branches sway, wild and free.

Butterflies prance in a joyful flight,
They twirl and spin in pure delight.
The flowers chuckle, bright and bold,
With stories of sunshine yet untold.

Crickets hum a merry tune,
As shadows stretch by the light of the moon.
In every rustle and fluttering sound,
Nature's giggles truly abound.

The brook chuckles as it splashes,
While petals float in joyful clashes.
With each turn of the season's grace,
Nature wears a laughing face.

Quiet Chuckles in the Grove

In the grove where shadows play,
Little creatures find their way.
Frogs in hats, they leap and bound,
Mirth and mischief all around.

Birds croon sweet with notes so bright,
Their melodies bring pure delight.
A rabbit slips on dewy grass,
Laughter follows as they pass.

The trees whisper secrets, soft and low,
Buddies sharing just so they know.
Each leaf shuffles with a grin,
A chorus of joy begins within.

Sunsets paint the sky in flair,
While fireflies twinkle, light as air.
In this playful, leafy space,
You'll find echoes of nature's grace.

Jovial Roots

Roots entwined with stories grand,
A tapestry beneath the land.
They chuckle softly as they grow,
In secret whispers, their tales flow.

Pinecones drop with playful thuds,
They bounce around like little buds.
The acorns giggle, as they roll,
Each one dreaming, a tiny goal.

Raccoons scamper with cheeky haste,
They tease the shadows, show their taste.
With every rustle, fun abounds,
In the depths where laughter sounds.

Dancing leaves in the crisp blue air,
Nature's joy, beyond compare.
Each root and branch a jester's hand,
In this whimsical, lively land.

The Joyful Audio of Understory

In the understory, whispers gleam,
Frogs croak jokes, or so it seems.
The undergrowth, a stage so bright,
With giggling sounds, a pure delight.

Mushrooms peek with curious caps,
They share wise tales of nature's maps.
As shadows dance in sprightly pairs,
Each twirl brings laughter up the stairs.

Honeybees buzz with a cheerful tone,
In search of nectar, never alone.
Their sweet melodies float on by,
A joyful hum beneath the sky.

So pause a moment, hear the glee,
Of nature's voice, wild and free.
In every rustle and gentle sweep,
The forest's laughter is ours to keep.

Whimsy in the Wind's Gentle Breath

A gentle breeze plays peek-a-boo,
As swirling greens dance with a view.
Nature giggles, a soft serenade,
In every rustle, joy is displayed.

Squirrels chase, they leap and bound,
While shadows jig on the warm, dry ground.
Small critters play tag in their game,
Whispers of mischief call each name.

A puddle reflects the sky's blue grin,
Where curious frogs jump and spin.
Each tickle of grass, a friendly nudge,
Every moment calls for a warm, soft judge.

Beneath the tree, the sun starts to peek,
In vibrant hues, the world feels sleek.
The joyous sound of nature's cheer,
In every flutter, smiles appear.

The Revelry of Leafy Revelations

Leaves tumble down like whispers of cheer,
Hiding giggles the forest holds dear.
A raccoon winks with a cheeky grin,
Under the boughs where adventures begin.

Acorns roll as squirrels take flight,
With pitter-pat paws, oh, what a sight!
Unruly branches sway with delight,
In a dance of shadows, pure and bright.

The sun flirts shy behind leafy curls,
As butterflies twirl, a flurry of twirls.
Crickets strum tunes on this merry stage,
While the woodland whispers a playful page.

Chasing the breeze, the petals collide,
In a humorous race, joy takes a ride.
Each flutter and flap, a tickle divine,
Where nature's laughter intertwines.

Ecstatic Whispers of the Woodland

In the heart of the woods, the whispers spread,
Of chortling leaves where the old tales thread.
An owl with a hat, perched high on a limb,
Underneath him, the shadows begin.

Hares in bow ties prance with style,
They giggle and hop in a playful pile.
The sun spills laughter through branches wide,
As secrets of whimsy in shadows hide.

A playful fox shows off his new kicks,
While beetles march to their own little tricks.
The brook bubbles up with a giggle or two,
As it splashes away with a hearty woohoo!

Dancing through glades with a magical spark,
Every corner alive, an echoing lark.
In this realm of fun, where spirits reside,
The woodland whispers, let joy be your guide.

Colorful Frolics Beneath the Sky

Beneath the expanse where the bright sun beams,
The world bursts alive, unraveling dreams.
With an explosion of color, each creature prances,
In the wind's soft giggling, the heart dances.

Tiny flutters of wings on a bright daffodil,
Mice in bowties, mischief at will.
Each leaf a canvas of stories retold,
In this joyous area where play is bold.

A lark sings sweetly, filling the air,
Frogs croak in rhythm, a chorus so rare.
Clouds play tag, painting smiles in the blue,
While shadows of laughter dance as they do.

As twilight descends, the giggles soften,
In a sunset's embrace, the day's frolics often.
Nature wraps tight in a blanket of glee,
In this carnival of life, forever carefree.

The Snicker of the Wild

In the woods where shadows dance,
The critters plot their silly prance.
Squirrels chirp, in playful tease,
While dancing leaves sway in the breeze.

A rabbit hops with a cheeky grin,
Joking with friends that they can't win.
The birds compose a song absurd,
Each chirp a laughter, not a word.

Raccoons wear masks as if to play,
Stealing the snacks from the folks all day.
While owls hoot with a comical twist,
Their giggles echo through the mist.

So nature's jesters frolic and tease,
In a world where joy will always please.

Happy Rustic Whimsy

A windmill spins with a silly shout,
Its blades are whipping, twirling about.
Chickens cluck in a merry fuss,
Chasing the sun, no time to rush.

Piglets roll in the grass so bright,
Creating mud pies, what a sight!
The farmer chuckles with his hat askew,
As ducks parade in a row, what a view!

Goats nibble close with playful bites,
While bees chase butterflies in delights.
The barnyard echoes with giggles loud,
Every creature feeling so proud.

The joy of rustic life we share,
Brings laughter floating in the air.

Cheerful Breezes' Embrace

A gust of fun sweeps through the glade,
Twisting the tresses of the shade.
Leaves chuckle softly, their colors bright,
As sunbeams wink, a playful sight.

Breezes tickle the flowers' cheeks,
In harmony, nature playfully speaks.
Grasshoppers leap with a jolly hop,
While daisies sway, never will they stop.

The world spins round in a jolly tune,
Under a friendly, smiling moon.
With every puff, a ticklish cheer,
The cheerful air wraps us near.

In this embrace of blissful days,
We dance with joy in countless ways.

The Festival of Foliage

Autumn arrives with a fluttering grin,
As leaves cascade, twirling within.
Pumpkins chuckle in their patchy crowd,
While hay bales wear their straw, so proud.

Merry folk gather, a sparkling sight,
With laughter echoing through the night.
Chestnuts roast, and cider flows,
In this festive scene, the spirit glows.

Fireflies twinkle, like stars so near,
Each flicker sharing a whimsical cheer.
Children dance with glee, so bright,
Creating memories in the starry light.

So lift a cup to the joyous breeze,
Celebrating nature's funny tease.

A Festival of Colors and Chuckles

Amidst the trees, a jolly cheer,
A symphony of giggles, bright and clear.
Crimson, gold, and pumpkin pie,
As whispers swirl, the shades fly high.

From branches shake, a playful breeze,
Tickling toes and dancing leaves.
The sun peeks through with cheeky delight,
While shadows play hide and seek in flight.

Autumn's art, a canvas bright,
Each leaf a smile, a joyous sight.
Join in the fun, let spirits thieve,
In nature's gallery, we laugh and weave.

With every crunch, a secret shared,
In colors bold, we are unpaired.
The trees stand tall, join in the jest,
A festival of color, truly blessed.

Rustle and Roar of Leafy Laughter

The forest shakes with mirth today,
As leaves in frolic jump and sway.
Breezy giggles twist and twine,
With every rustle, joy is divine.

Acorns tumble, a jolly game,
Wobbling folks without shame.
With nature's charm, we twist and shout,
Each crack and pop a fun-filled bout.

Squirrels race on branches high,
While chubby chipmunks zip on by.
The leafy laughter echoes near,
Whispers of joy, a song to hear.

A tapestry of joy so grand,
In every inch of leafy land.
We'll dance and prance, a merry throng,
In nature's arms, we'll all belong.

The Elation of Earth's Ticking Clock

The clock ticks wild, the seasons spin,
With every tick, the giggles begin.
Chasing time through vibrant hues,
As autumn weaves its funny clues.

Dancing shadows, a playful show,
Where rabbits hop and breezes blow.
Time's a jester, making haste,
While chuckles swirl, a funny taste.

The pumpkin patch, a joyful sight,
Where laughter gleams in golden light.
The earth spins round, a quirky spin,
Where smiles abound and grins begin.

Here's to the hours that tick and tock,
Where every moment sparks the clock.
In this whimsical, bright parade,
The joy of time can't be betrayed.

Mirthful Memories in the Woodland Wild

In woods alive with tales and cheer,
Each tree holds stories, crystal clear.
Through rustling leaves, a spirit flies,
With glimmers of joy and laughing ties.

From shimmering shades, the tales unfold,
Of furry friends and pranks retold.
With every turn, a custom spin,
As woodland creatures join the din.

Crickets chirp a merry tune,
While dancing shadows sway like a boon.
The air is thick with laughter's song,
In nature's cradle, we all belong.

Each step we take through vibrant lands,
Is threaded tight with joyful strands.
So here we play, so wild and free,
In woodland wild, pure jubilee.

www.ingramcontent.com/pod-product-compliance
Lightning Source LLC
Chambersburg PA
CBHW051649160426
43209CB00004B/847